START-A-CRAFT

Fabric Painting

Get started in a new craft with easy-to-follow

projects for beginners

MELANIE WILLIAMS

CHARTWELL
BOOKS. INC

A QUINTET BOOK

Published by Chartwell Books
A Division of Book Sales, Inc.
110 Enterprise Avenue
Secaucus, New Jersey 07094

This edition produced for sale in the U.S.A.,
its territories and dependencies only.

ISBN 0—7858—0061—1

This book was designed and produced by
Quintet Publishing Limited
6 Blundell Street
London N7 9BH

Creative Director: Richard Dewing
Designers: Ian Hunt and Linda Henley
Senior Editor: Laura Sandelson
Editor: Lydia Darbyshire
Photographer: Paul Forrester

Typeset in Great Britain by
Central Southern Typesetters, Eastbourne
Manufactured in Hong Kong by
Regent Publishing Services Limited
Printed in China

ACKNOWLEDGEMENT
The publishers would like to thank
Dylon International Limited for supplying
the fabric paints used to make up the projects
for photography.

Contents

Introduction

Painting on fabric offers you the opportunity to create sensational effects on ordinary household items. Liven up a dull T-shirt or an old pair of jeans; design table linen to match your china, monogrammed bed linen, cushions to match your wallpaper and loads of other exciting things.

You don't have to be a great artist to master the art of fabric painting; many simple and effective designs can be done free-style. As your skills develop, you can attempt more ambitious designs which require a steady hand, such as copying a motif from a book or magazine, or even making up your own design and transferring it to fabric.

There are numerous ways of applying the paint to the fabric. Stenciling is an excellent way of covering a large area or creating a repeat pattern, for example on a tablecloth. Printing with sliced vegetables, fruit, and flowers is a novel way of creating abstract patterns to fabric — and it's easy: simply apply paint to the surface or edge of the object with which you are painting and print it directly on the fabric. Throughout the book there are projects that incorporate masking, sponging, printing, and painting on dark fabric so you become familiar with a whole range of fabric painting techniques.

Fabric paints come in many forms so you can create many different effects with puff, glitter, and pearlized paint. Colors can be easily mixed and applied to both natural and synthetic material. Furthermore, by ironing newly painted fabric on the wrong side, the article becomes colorfast, which means that it can be machine-washed time and time again. For best results new fabrics should be washed and ironed before paint is applied so that any dressing which would prevent the paint from being absorbed is removed. Remember always to place a piece of paper underneath the fabric onto which you are painting.

This book is especially designed for beginners: no expensive equipment is needed, nor any special skills. Although suggestions have been given for colors and designs in all the projects, there is no reason why you shouldn't try different combinations of colors and patterns. In many of the projects, there are illustrations of alternate ways of painting the items to encourage you to use your imagination and, more important, to have fun with the paints.

Basic equipment you will need for painting on fabric.

Painted Espadrilles

Plain espadrilles come in a variety of bright colors, and they are inexpensive to buy. Decorating lighter colors – pale blue, green, pink, and white – tends to be more successful than applying paint to darker shades. I have suggested using masking tape as a guide, but you may feel confident enough to apply the paint free-style.

You will need
◊ 1 pair of plain espadrilles
◊ Newspaper
◊ Masking tape
◊ Scissors
◊ Fabric paints (I used red, yellow, and blue)
◊ Mixing palette
◊ Brushes (small and medium sizes)
◊ Tailor's chalk or colored pencil)
◊ Iron
◊ Cloth

1 Put some crumpled-up newspaper into each espadrille so that the surface is smooth and taut.

2 Place three strips of masking tape across the front of the shoe, varying the distance between the pieces or using narrower tape if you want narrower or wider lines.

3 Begin with the blue paint and use short strokes to paint the first stripe. Do not water down the paint or it will run.

4 When you have painted the red and yellow stripes, leave the paint to dry before removing the masking tape.

5 Add the details to the stripes.

6 I added bumps to give a wavy effect; this can be done free-style.

7 Use tailor's chalk or a colored pencil to draw a pattern of random circles on the sides of each espadrille.

8 Paint in the circles using a small brush to give a neat outline.

9 Place a piece of cloth over the espadrille and iron to seal the paint.

Customized Jeans

This project is an ideal way of experimenting with some of the more specialized fabric paints that are available these days — puff, glitter, and fluorescent paints, for example. It is also a great way to liven up an old pair of jeans, and there are endless possibilities to try.

You will need
◊ Pair of jeans
◊ Newspaper
◊ Fabric paints (including puff, glitter, and fluorescent)
◊ Mixing palette
◊ Paint brushes (various sizes)
◊ Hair dryer

1 Place a few sheets of newspaper inside the jeans to protect them from paint seeping through.

2 Use puff paint to draw zigzag lines around the pockets.

3 Add green dots to the inside of the zigzags.

4 Paint on a patch using a mixture of yellow and white. Draw on some crosshatched squares using a mixture of blue and purple paint.

7 Add green puff paint crosses inside the heart and white dots around the edge. Add more patches down the legs of the jeans if you wish. When the paint is completely dry, puff it up using a hair dryer.

5 Paint "stitches" around the patch using pink puff paint.

6 Draw another motif on the other leg of the jeans — a pink heart, for example. Use green puff paint to draw a border around the heart.

Butterfly T-Shirt

Plain T-shirts in a wide range of colors and sizes are available all over the place, and many of them cost very little. Alternatively, you could give a new lease of life to an old T-shirt. I have drawn a butterfly design, but there is no limit to the patterns and motifs that you can try. This is an ideal project for experimenting with some of the specialized fabric paints, such as glitter paints, and puff paints, which change when they are exposed to the warmth of a hair dryer.

You will need
◊ Tracing paper
◊ Pencil
◊ Scissors
◊ Plain T-shirt
◊ Newspaper
◊ Pins
◊ Tailor's chalk or colored pencil
◊ Fabric paints (including puff and glitter paints)
◊ Mixing palette
◊ Paintbrushes (various sizes)
◊ Hair dryer

1 Trace the butterfly template from the outline on page 45 and cut it out. Cut out the holes in the wings.

2 Put newspaper inside the T-shirt to stop paint from seeping through. Pin the template to the front of the T-shirt and draw around the shape with a colored pencil or tailor's chalk. Use a colored pencil to add other details – the antennae, for example – freehand.

3 Paint in the wings using whatever colors you wish. Use a fine paintbrush for the small dots and a ¼ inch brush for the larger ones.

4 Add other colors. Allow the paint to dry for about 20 minutes before painting another color next to it.

5 Add lines of puff paint around the patterns on the wings.

6 Add some spots of glitter paint around the neckline.

7 Outline the wing shapes in a different color puff paint. Puff up the paint using a hair dryer.

Abstract Patterns

This is an ideal way of decorating lengths of solid fabric so that you can make them up into curtains, table linen, pillow covers, or even clothes. Look around your home and you are sure to find countless bits and pieces — sponges, combs, jar lids, pen tops, — that can be used to make interesting patterns. You could also experiment with food — pasta or potatoes, for example — to create some unusual designs.

You will need
◊ Items for printing — combs, wooden spools, pen tops, etc.
◊ Newspaper
◊ Fabric
◊ Masking tape
◊ Fabric paint
◊ Mixing palette
◊ Paintbrush (medium size)
◊ Iron
◊ Cloth

1 Assemble the items you think would make interesting shapes. You might find it helpful to make a rough sketch of your overall design before you begin.

2 Cover your work surface with newspaper and lay out the fabric. Use masking tape to keep it in position if necessary.

3 Mix the colors you want to use in a palette.

4 Apply paint to the object — I used a comb — taking care not to use too much paint or the outline will not look crisp and neat.

7 Incorporate the shape into your design. Leave to dry.

8 Use a different color on your next object. I used a small piece of sponge, which gives an interesting and uneven texture.

9 Leave the third color to dry before you apply the next series of colored shapes. When you are satisfied with the pattern, iron under a cloth to set the paints.

5 Use the comb to transfer the paint to the fabric. Continue all around the edge of the fabric, then leave to dry for about 20 minutes.

6 Take your next object – I used a wooden spool – and paint the surface with a different color.

Vegetable-printed Apron

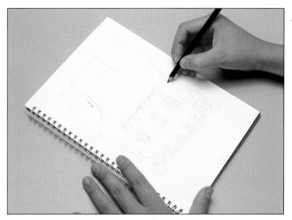

Vegetables that have a distinctive shape, such as cabbage, mushrooms, chili, and broccoli, are ideal for fabric printing. Cut them in half and use them to decorate a muslin apron of the kind you can buy in catering or do-it-yourself stores. Try experimenting with halved fruit.

You will need
◊ Selection of vegetables (broccoli, mushrooms, cabbage, okra, chili, etc.)
◊ Kitchen knife
◊ Pencil
◊ Typing paper
◊ Plain muslin apron
◊ Newspaper
◊ Fabric paints
◊ Mixing palette
◊ Paintbrush (medium size)
◊ Fabric paint pens
◊ Iron
◊ Cloth

4 Test the cabbage on a piece of rough paper to check that the surface is smooth and gives an even impression. You will need to press fairly hard to get a good print, but do not put too much paint on the vegetable or the pattern will smudge.

1 Cut the vegetables you want to include in your design in half with a sharp knife. Include the stalks and cut more than one of each so that you can use several colors.

2 Draw a rough sketch on typing paper of how you want the apron to look.

3 Lay the apron on sheets of newspaper and prepare the paints. Use a paintbrush to paint the surface of, say, the cabbage.

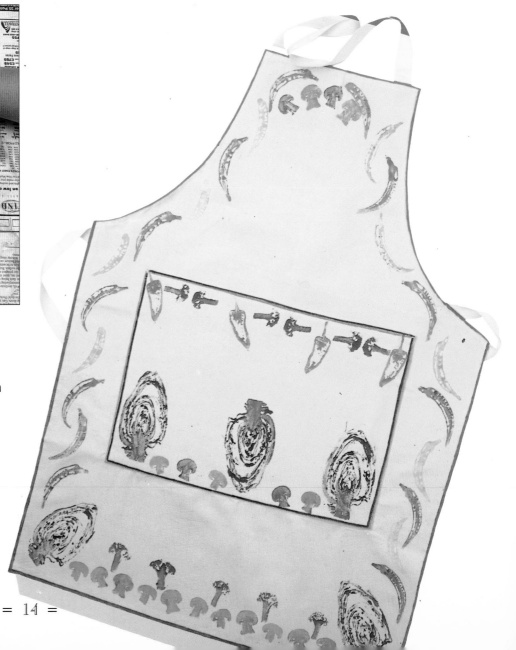

5 Print the cabbage on the apron.

6 Add more vegetable prints to build up your design, taking care not to move the vegetable as you apply pressure. Add fresh paint for every print.

7 Use a fabric marker pen to draw a line around the edge of the apron and to highlight the pocket edge. Iron under a cloth to set the paints.

Printing with Flowers

This simple project uses flowers and leaves to decorate fabric, which could be used for pillow covers, table or bed linen, or even curtains. Some kinds of plant material work better than others — flowers and leaves with sturdy, unfussy outlines give more successful prints than more delicate shapes. Try buddleia, ivy, and conifer leaves and flowers such as daisies. The backs of leaves with prominent veins work especially well.

You will need
◊ Rough paper
◊ Colored pencils
◊ Newspaper
◊ Fabric of your choice
◊ Masking tape
◊ A selection of flowers and leaves
◊ Fabric paints
◊ Mixing palette
◊ Paintbrush (medium size)
◊ Iron
◊ Cloth

1 Position the flowers and leaves in a pleasing design. Make a rough sketch of the design and color in the shapes so that you have a reference when you start to print.

2 Cover your work surface with newspaper and spread out your fabric, taping it in position if necessary. Mix your paints and paint some of the leaves.

3 Using your sketch as reference, place a leaf on the fabric, pressing it firmly but gently. Hold it down for 10 seconds, then raise an edge to see if the impression has printed. If you are happy with the result, carefully lift the leaf to avoid smudging the paint. Continue building up the design with other leaves.

4 Now paint a flower, placing it as indicated on your rough sketch. Fill in any gaps in the design, and don't worry if some of the flowers look rather abstract. Leave to dry before ironing under a cloth to set the paints.

Folk Art Picture

This charming image is achieved by applying a series of stencils, one after the other, and painting each in a different color. You could frame the completed image, as I have done, or you could paint two and make a pair of pillow covers.

You will need
◊ Tracing paper
◊ Pencil
◊ Stencil card
◊ Masking tape
◊ Craft knife
◊ Piece of canvas or muslin, approximately 11 × 13 inches
◊ Scissors
◊ Newspaper
◊ Stencil brush (¼ inch or ½ inch)
◊ Fabric paint
◊ Mixing palette
◊ Iron
◊ Cloth
◊ 4 buttons

3 Cut out a piece of canvas or muslin, and place it on some sheets of newspaper. Tape the first stencil – the background to the picture – securely in position over the canvas and paint it – I used blue. Carefully remove the stencil so that you do not smudge the edges. Leave to dry for a few minutes.

4 Tape the second stencil – the house front and chimney piece – accurately in position and apply dark blue paint. Use a paintbrush to paint around the window areas.

1 Trace the stencil designs on pages 46 to 48, drawing each of the outlines onto equal-sized sheets of paper so that they will all fit together accurately.

2 Tape each traced stencil onto a separate piece of stencil card, taking care to position each outline in the same position on each piece of card. Cut out the holes in each stencil.

5 Leave the paint to dry before you use the next stencil.

6 Tape the next stencil – the front door and roof – in place. This time use brown paint. Again, leave it to dry.

7 Tape the next stencil in place and then paint the side of the house purple. Leave it to dry before using the last stencil, the foreground and trees, which are painted green.

8 Iron under a cloth to set the paint and sew a button in each corner.

Child's Wall-hanging

This charming parade of stenciled animals would look great on a child's bedroom wall. The project uses simple, colorful hand-stitching and stenciling, which combine to give an old-fashioned, slightly folksy effect. You could make a similar piece using numbers or letters instead of animals.

You will need
◊ Tracing paper
◊ Pencils
◊ Stencil card
◊ Masking tape
◊ Craft knife
◊ 8 pieces of cream-colored fabric, each measuring approximately 5 × 5 inches
◊ Fabric paints
◊ Mixing palette
◊ Stencil brushes ¼ inch and ½ inch
◊ Sponge (natural sponge is best)
◊ Iron
◊ Cloth
◊ 2 pieces of colored fabric, each measuring approximately 8 × 50 inches (I used blue)
◊ Pins
◊ Scissors
◊ Needle
◊ Colored embroidery thread
◊ 2 buttons
◊ Bias binding, tape or ribbon, approximately 4 inches

1 Trace the eight animal shapes from pages 44 and 45. Place each animal tracing on a piece of stencil card and hold it in place with masking tape.

2 Use a craft knife to cut out each shape. Discard the tracing paper.

3 Cut out eight squares of cream-colored fabric.

4 Use masking tape to hold each cutout animal in position on a square of fabric.

= 18 =

5 Prepare your paints, then color the pig's body using a stencil brush.

6 Color the pig's feet brown and add a band of brown across its body.

7 The rooster has a blue-green body and a bright red comb.

8 Add some yellow and orange to the feathers in the rooster's tail.

9 Color the cow's body black and its hooves and udder pink. Make some spots by sponging on some white paint.

10 Paint the rest of the animals, using the photograph of the finished wall hanging as a guide. Turn under the edges of each square and iron under a cloth to set the colors and press down the turned-back edges.

11 Place the two rectangles of fabric together and pin. Space the eight animal pictures evenly along one of the long rectangles of fabric, pinning them in position.

12 Use colored embroidery threads to straight stitch each square in place.

13 Turn under the edge of the large rectangle to make a neat hem on the front and hand sew with yellow embroidery thread.

14 Sew a button in each of the top corners and add loops of tape, bias binding or ribbon from which to hang it.

Marine Lampshade

Fabric paints can be used to decorate a plain lampshade to suit your own home furnishings. Plain, straight-sided lampshades are available in most do-it-yourself stores and large department stores, and they are not too expensive.
I have used simple sponging and stenciling techniques to create this peaceful underwater scene.

1 Sketch a rough plan of your ideas on plain paper before you begin.

2 Use a marker pen to draw the seaweed, fish, and starfish shapes onto stencil card. If you prefer, draw the outlines in pencil first as a guide.

3 Use a craft knife to cut out the shapes.

4 Cut the card into individual stencils.

5 Mix your colors and use an artist's sponge or a bath sponge cut into small pieces to start filling in the background of the design. Begin with a light layer of blue,

then add a second layer to darken the tone gradually as it nears the top of the shade.

You will need
◊ Paper
◊ Pencil
◊ Marker pen
◊ Stencil card
◊ Craft knife
◊ Scissors
◊ Plain lampshade
◊ Fabric paints
◊ Sponge (natural sponge is best)
◊ Masking tape
◊ Stencil brush ¼ inch or ½ inch

6 Add yellow around the bottom to represent sand. Leave to dry for about 20 minutes.

7 Tape the starfish stencil in position, referring to your sketch as a guide. Hold the lampshade firmly and use a stencil brush to color the starfish red. Repeat until there is a series of starfish around the rim.

8 Tape the seaweed stencil in position and paint it green. Repeat the motif around the base but using different shades of green.

9 Next tape one of the fish stencils in place. Use different colors — I used blue, purple, and red — and continue until there is a school of fish swimming all around the shade.

10 Paint in some free-style air bubbles.

Shopping Bag

The combination of the attractive fruit design and the durable nature of this simple canvas drawstring bag makes it the perfect way to carry heavy fruit and vegetables home from the market. Although I have supplied simple templates for the motifs, you could decorate it with a different pattern so that the bag could be used to carry school things or your sport gear.

1 Trace the fruit motifs from the templates on page 43 and cut out.

2 Cut two pieces of canvas. Place the templates on the canvas, pin them in position, and use a pencil to draw around the outlines.

3 Use your traced outlines as a guide to fill in the details of the fruit.

4 Use a ruler to add the gingham-checked tablecloth pattern.

5 Mix your paints. You will need yellow for the bananas, purple for the grapes (you can add some white, yellow, and orange for a lighter shade of purple), and green for the apples.

You will need
◊ Tracing paper
◊ Pencil
◊ Scissors
◊ 2 pieces of canvas, each 16 × 18 inches
◊ Pins
◊ Ruler
◊ Fabric paint
◊ Mixing palette

◊ Paintbrushes (3 sizes)
◊ Fabric paint pen (blue)
◊ Iron
◊ Cloth
◊ Sewing machine
◊ Sewing thread
◊ ¼ inch cord, 30 inches long
◊ Safety pin

6 Use short strokes to apply the first color. Aim to create a three-dimensional effect.

7 Paint the apples and bananas.

8 Color the stalks and leaves of the apples.

9 Add the detail to the grapes, using dark green for the tendrils and brown for the stalks.

10 Add detail in brown to the bananas to make them look as natural as possible. Leave

the paint to dry for about 20 minutes, then iron under a cloth.

11 Paint in the white squares of the tablecloth border pattern and outline the squares with a blue fabric painting pen.

12 Color in alternate squares and leave to dry for about 20 minutes. Iron under a cloth. Decorate the second piece of canvas in the same way if you wish.

13 With right sides together, machine-stitch one side of the bag.

14 Open the bag so that the middle inside seam faces you. On each side at the top, turn 2 inches of the raw edge in at an angle. Machine-stitch into place. Fold back the bag with right sides together and machine-stitch along the bottom and side. Turn right side out.

15 Use a safety pin to thread the cord through as a drawstring. Bind the ends of the cord to keep it from unraveling.

Napkins

These crisp, attractive napkins would be ideal for an outdoor meal or a summer dinner party. You could use the same motifs to decorate a matching tablecloth, too, or you could devise your own motifs or color schemes to decorate some napkins for Christmas, Easter, or a birthday theme party.

You will need
◊ Tracing paper
◊ Pencil
◊ Scissors
◊ 4—6 squares of fabric, each measuring approximately 14 × 14 inches
◊ Pins
◊ Colored pencil
◊ Ruler
◊ Tailor's chalk
◊ Fabric paints
◊ Mixing palette
◊ Paintbrushes (small and medium sizes)
◊ Iron
◊ Cloth
◊ Sewing machine
◊ Sewing thread

1 Draw a free-style watermelon slice on a plate and cut it out.

2 Cut out the squares of fabric and pin the illustration to one piece, placing it in the center of the fabric. Use a colored pencil – or if your fabric is dark, use a white pencil – and a ruler to draw the checked border on the top and bottom edges of the square. The border should be about 1 inch wide.

3 Use tailor's chalk or a colored pencil to draw around the template. Using a mixture of white and red, paint the flesh of the watermelon pink. Highlight the edges with white paint.

4 Paint the rind, first with light green, then with a darker green.

5 Add the seeds with black paint, highlighting them with white.

6 Use white paint for the plate.

7 Add a blue-green checked border to the plate, painting the squares free-style.

8 Paint alternate squares of the border with white and blue-green paint. Iron under a cloth to set the color.

9 Use a sewing machine to hem the edges.

Animal Pillows

Scatter these lively animal pillows on a child's bed or arrange them in a group on a chair. Watered-down fabric paints have been used to achieve the background colors, while thicker paints are used for the detailed markings. Simple embroidery stitches in brightly colored threads have been added to enhance the details of feathers, whiskers, and so on.

You will need
◊ Tracing paper
◊ Pencil
◊ Scissors
◊ Pins
◊ White cotton fabric, approximately 10 × 20 inches for each pillow
◊ Newspaper
◊ Fabric paints
◊ Mixing palette
◊ Paintbrushes (small and medium)
◊ Colored embroidery threads
◊ Needle
◊ Sewing thread
◊ Sewing machine
◊ Polyester stuffing
◊ Buttons for eyes
◊ String for pig's tail

1 Trace the animal templates on pages 40 to 42 and cut out.

2 Pin each template to a double layer of fabric and cut around it.

3 Place each animal shape on some newspaper and prepare your paints.

4 Water down the paints that you are going to use for the background – for example, use

orange for the cat – but do not make the color flat; it will look more natural if it is streaky.

5 Add spots on the back and head and a nose and tail, using the photograph on page 31 as a guide.

6 Make the pig in the same way and remember to include two ears.

7 Use brown paint for the pig's feet and the spots on its flanks.

8 The rooster is more difficult. The background is a combination of green, purple, pink, and yellow. Apply each color separately, but try to achieve a soft, feathery effect with no harsh edges to the colors.

9 Add a yellow beak and bright red comb.

10 Iron both sides of each of the animals under a cloth when you have finished them to set the paints.

11 Use embroidery threads to stitch details on the rooster's neck feathers.

12 Stitch some additional feather detailing on the rooster's back.

13 Stitch around the spots on the cat and embroider the whiskers. Remember to stitch the cat's paws.

14 Pin the two pieces of the pillow together and machine-stitch around the edge, leaving about 2 inches open along the bottom edge.

15 Carefully clip the curved edges up the stitching line so that the seams lie flat.

16 Turn the pillow right side out, using the wooden end of a paintbrush to push out the seams, especially around the rooster's beak and comb. Stuff the pillow, pushing the filling into the head and tail with a piece of wooden dowel or the wrong end of a knitting needle.

17 Sew up the open seam. Repeat steps 14–17 for the pig and cat.

18 Stitch on buttons for eyes and remember to add the pig's ears.

19 Make a tail for the pig by painting some string pink and sewing it onto the pig's back.

Pillowcases

Simple stenciling techniques allow you to decorate plain cotton pillowcases with a fresh floral design, and once you have mastered the techniques, there is no need to stop at pillowcases: you can decorate a duvet cover and sheet to match. I have supplied templates for the flowers, but you may prefer to design your own motifs.

You will need
◊ Marker pen
◊ Tracing paper
◊ Masking tape
◊ Stencil card
◊ Craft knife
◊ 2 plain cotton pillowcases
◊ Newspaper
◊ Fabric paint
◊ Mixing palette
◊ Stencil brush
◊ Iron
◊ Cloth

1 Use a marker pen to trace the stencil patterns from the outlines on page 38.

2 Use masking tape to hold the traced shapes securely in position on the stencil card.

3 Cut around the shapes with a craft knife, working on a cutting mat or a piece of thick cardboard. Discard the tracing paper.

4 Put some pieces of newspaper inside the pillowcase to protect the other side from any paint that seeps through.

5 Position the stem templates on the pillowcase, securing them with masking tape.

6 Mix the paint colors. Paint the stems with a small (¼-inch) stencil brush using different shades of green.

You could paint them all the same color or in various shades of red — add orange, yellow, or purple, for example.

11 Allow the paint to dry, then iron with a piece of cloth over the paint to set the colors.

7 Dab rather than using brush strokes for a "sponging" effect and take care not to splash paint onto the rest of the pillowcase.

8 Repeat until there are stems across the pillowcase — about eight in all. Remove the stencils.

9 Position the leaf stencils and secure them with masking tape. Color the leaves as you did the stems, holding the stencil firmly down with your fingers so that paint does not run under the cut edge.

10 Position the flower stencils and hold them in place with masking tape.

Doll

This simple doll makes a delightful gift for a child over five or six years old. You could design a different outfit if you preferred, or you could base the doll's appearance on someone you know. If you wish, you could add extra details such as a hair ribbon, a hat or a piece of jewelery.

You will need
◊ Sketch pad
◊ Colored pencils
◊ Tracing paper
◊ Pencil
◊ Piece of white fabric, 10 × 13 inches
◊ Pins
◊ Scissors
◊ Newspapers
◊ Polyester stuffing
◊ Sewing machine
◊ Sewing thread
◊ Fabric paints
◊ Mixing palette
◊ Paintbrushes (various sizes)
◊ Iron
◊ Cloth
◊ Needle
◊ Buttons

1 Sketch a design for your doll's clothes, keeping to the shape of the doll.

2 Trace the doll's template from page 39 and cut out. Fold the white fabric in half (so that it measures 5 × 13 inches) and pin the template to it, making sure that the pins go through both layers. Cut out the outline, adding a seam allowance of 1/8 inch all around.

3 Using your sketch as a reference, pencil guidelines on the cutout doll – hairline, top, pants, shoes, and so on. Add the details to front and back.

4 Cover your work surface with newspaper and paint the front of the doll. Begin with the background color of the blouse – I used blue.

5 Next paint in the shoes and pants and then the mouth, cheeks, and hair.

6 Allow the paint to dry, then add details such as the flower pattern to the top and the ruffles around the neck and pants.

7 Paint the face pale pink and leave to dry. Paint the back of the doll to match. Iron.

8 Place the two pieces, right sides together, and machine stitch all the way around the doll, leaving a gap of about 2 inches under one arm. Carefully clip the curves up to the sewing line at the neck, between the legs, and at the ends of the arms and legs so that the seams lie smoothly.

9 Turn the doll right side out. You may find it helpful to use the wrong end of a paintbrush to push the arms and legs through. Stuff the doll, adding little pinches at a time and using a piece of wooden dowel or the wrong end of a knitting needle to push the filler down into the arms and legs. Stitch up the underarm seam opening.

10 Sew on buttons for the eyes.

11 Paint on the eyebrows.

Herb Sachet

Scented sachets make ideal gifts. They can be hung among clothes in a wardrobe
or placed in drawers where they will delicately perfume your clothes. I have
shown how to paint a very simple design, but you may feel ambitious enough to
attempt a more detailed and realistic floral pattern using several colors.

You will need
- ◊ Piece of white cotton, approximately 6 × 8½ inches
- ◊ Piece of pale-colored cotton, 3 × 3½ inches (I used green)
- ◊ Scissors
- ◊ Pencil
- ◊ Fabric paint
- ◊ Mixing palette
- ◊ 2 brushes (small)
- ◊ Iron
- ◊ Cloth
- ◊ Pins
- ◊ Sewing thread
- ◊ Sewing machine
- ◊ Lace trim, approximately 8½ inches long
- ◊ Scissors
- ◊ 2 buttons
- ◊ ¼-inch- wide ribbon, approximately 10 inches
- ◊ Dried lavender

1 Cut out the pieces of white and colored fabrics and put the white material to one side.

2 Draw the lavender flower pattern on the colored fabric.

3 Paint in the outlines you have drawn, allow the paint to dry, then iron the painted pattern under a cloth.

4 Place the painted square at one end of the white cotton rectangle. Turn each edge under neatly approximately ¼ inch; pin and baste in place.

5 Use a sewing machine to stitch the square into position.

6 Turn over the top edge of the rectangle, pin, baste, and machine stitch into position. Fold the rectangle in two, with the painted piece on the inside and the short ends together. Sew along the bottom and along the open short edge. Stitch on the lace trim by hand. Turn right side out.

7 Sew the buttons on the front.

8 Catch the ribbon in position with a stitch or two at the side seam, fill the sachet with dried lavender, and tie the bow firmly.

Templates

PILLOWCASES

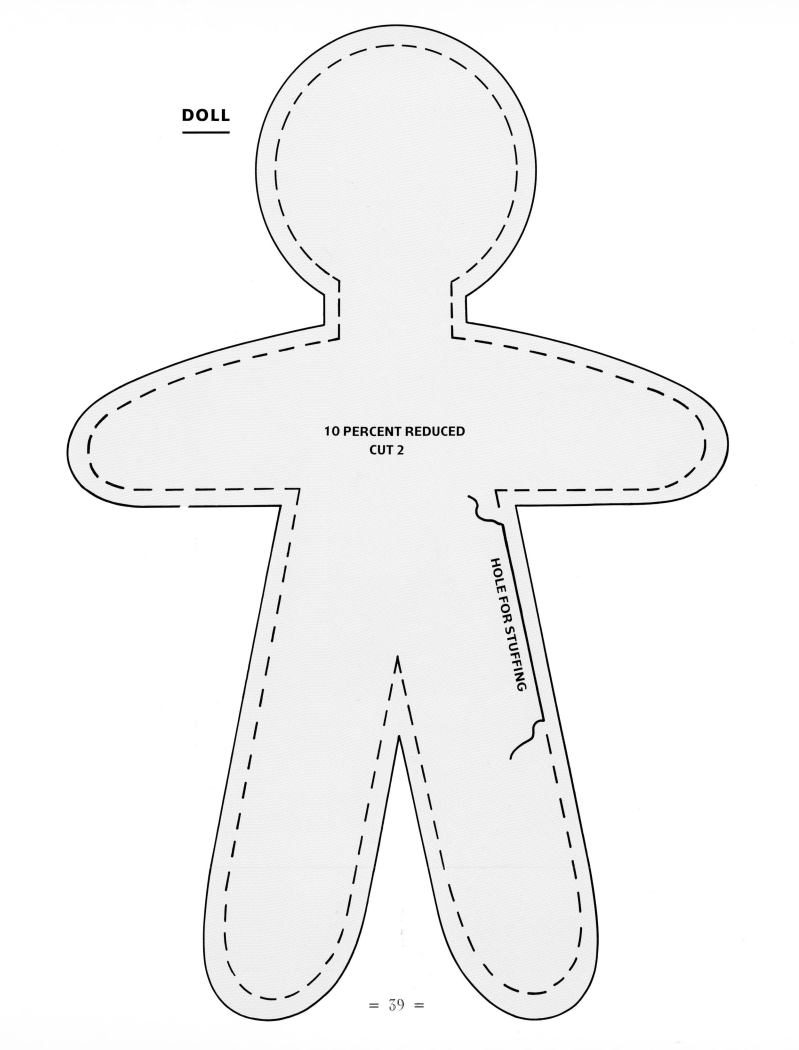

DOLL

10 PERCENT REDUCED
CUT 2

HOLE FOR STUFFING

ANIMAL PILLOWS

Pig's Ear
CUT 4

Pig
CUT 2

HOLE FOR STUFFING

ANIMAL PILLOWS

Chicken
CUT 2

HOLE FOR STUFFING

ANIMAL PILLOWS

Cat
CUT 2

HOLE FOR STUFFING

SHOPPING BAG

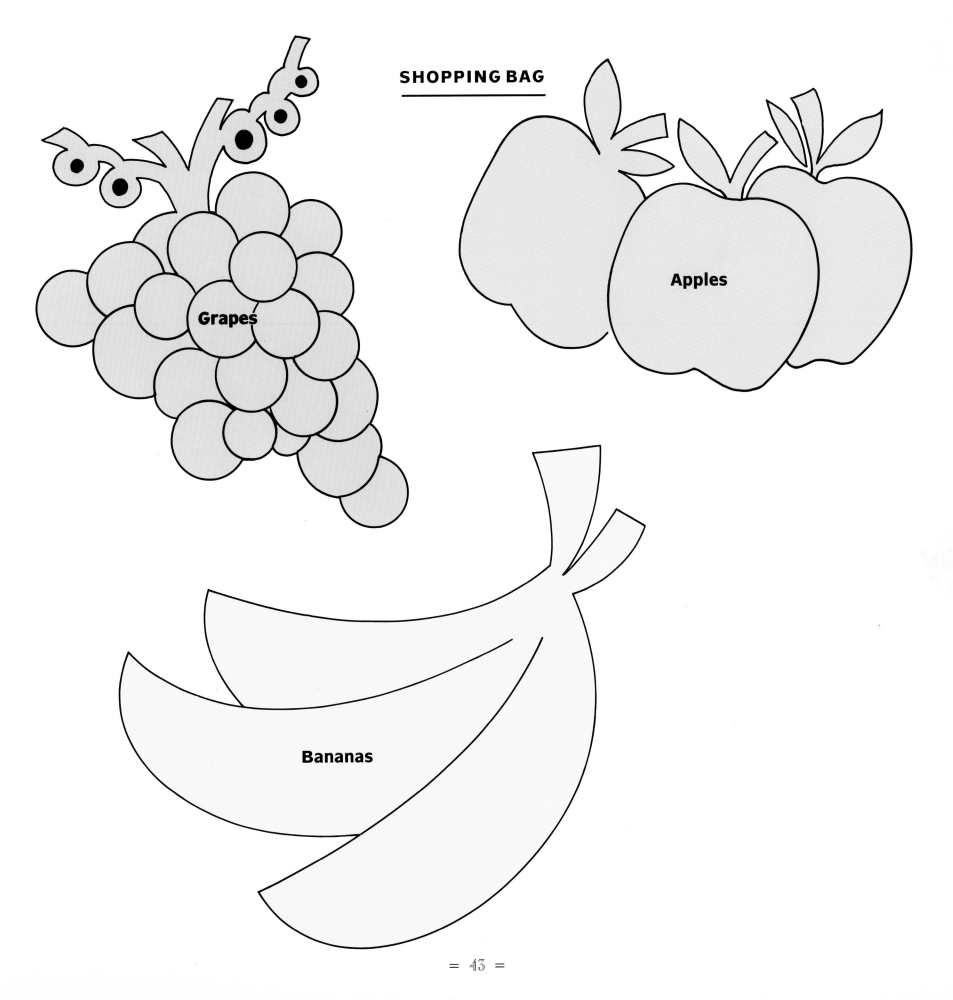

Grapes

Apples

Bananas

ANIMAL WALL HANGING

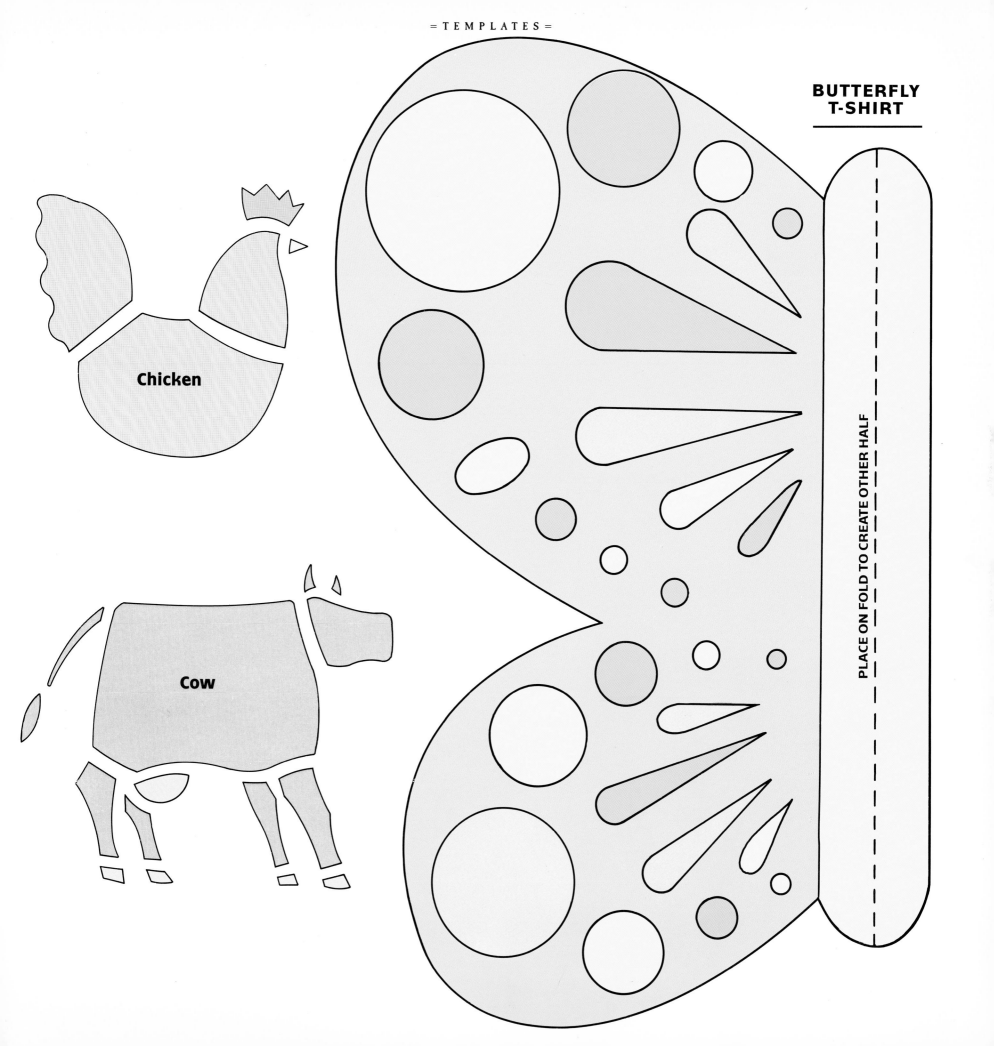

**BUTTERFLY
T-SHIRT**

PLACE ON FOLD TO CREATE OTHER HALF

Chicken

Cow

FOLK ART PICTURE

FOLK ART PICTURE

FOLK ART PICTURE

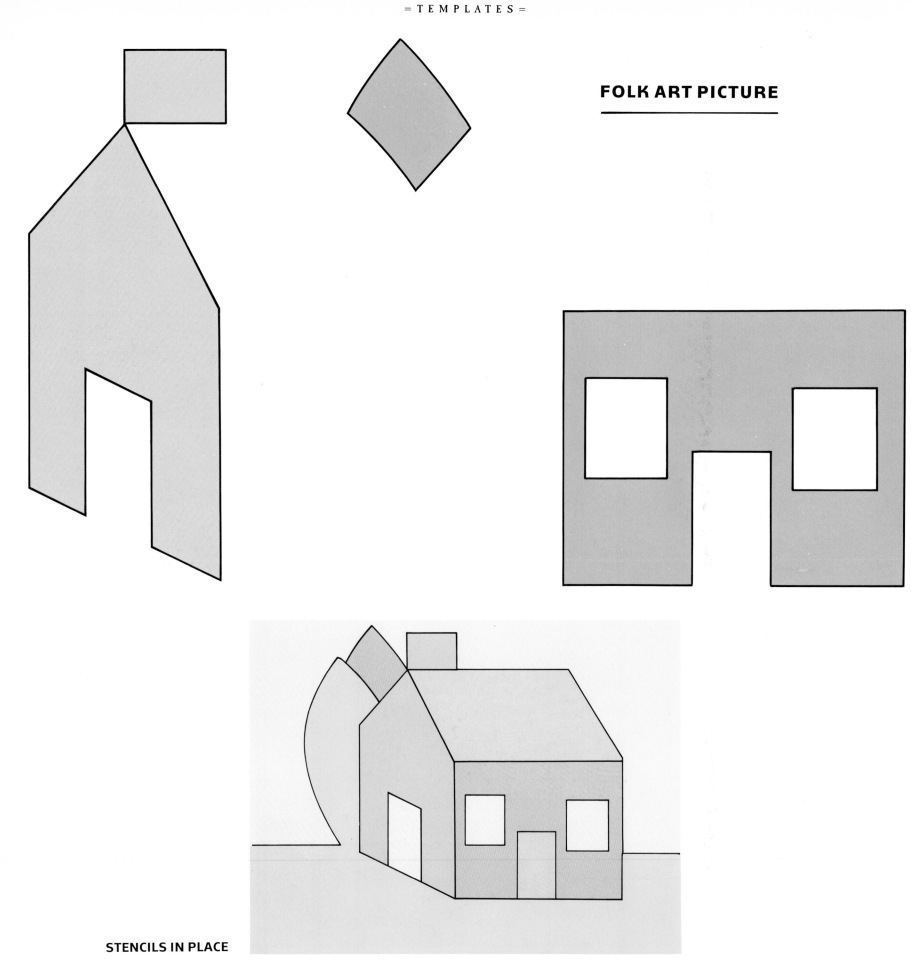

STENCILS IN PLACE